GREEN PARK

BY ELIAS JAMIESON BROWN

CURRENCY PRESS
The performing arts publisher

GRIFFIN
THEATRE
COMPANY

CURRENT THEATRE SERIES

First published in 2021
by Currency Press Pty Ltd,
PO Box 2287, Strawberry Hills, NSW, 2012, Australia
enquiries@currency.com.au
www.currency.com.au
in association with Griffin Theatre Company
Copyright: *Green Park* © Elias Jamieson Brown, 2021.

COPYING FOR EDUCATIONAL PURPOSES
The Australian *Copyright Act 1968* (Act) allows a maximum of one chapter or 10% of this book, whichever is the greater, to be copied by any educational institution for its educational purposes provided that that educational institution (or the body that administers it) has given a remuneration notice to Copyright Agency (CA) under the Act.
For details of the CA licence for educational institutions contact CA, 11/66 Goulburn Street, Sydney, NSW, 2000; tel: within Australia 1800 066 844 toll free; outside Australia 61 2 9394 7600; fax: 61 2 9394 7601; email: info@copyright.com.au

COPYING FOR OTHER PURPOSES
Except as permitted under the Act, for example a fair dealing for the purposes of study, research, criticism or review, no part of this book may be reproduced, stored in a retrieval system, or transmitted in any form or by any means without prior written permission. All enquiries should be made to the publisher at the address above.

Any performance or public reading of *Green Park* is forbidden unless a licence has been received from the author or the author's agent. The purchase of this book in no way gives the purchaser the right to perform the play in public, whether by means of a staged production or a reading. All applications for public performance should be addressed to the author c/- Currency Press

Typeset by Dean Nottle for Currency Press.
Cover image and design by Alphabet.
Cover features Elias Jamieson Brown.

Currency Press acknowledges the Traditional Owners of the Country on which we live and work. We pay our respects to all Aboriginal and Torres Strait Islander Elders, past and present.

 A catalogue record for this book is available from the National Library of Australia

Contents

GREEN PARK   1
Theatre Program at the end of the playtext

Green Park was first produced by Griffin Theatre Company at Green Park, Darlinghurst, on 5 February 2021, with the following cast:

    WARREN   Steve Le Marquand
    EDDEN   Joseph Althouse

Director and Dramaturg, Declan Greene
Designer, Emma White
Composer and Sound Designer, David Bergman
Writing Secondment, Riordan Berry
Stage Manager, Isabella Kerdijk

CHARACTERS

WARREN, mid-late 50s, scruffy and reserved
EDDEN, mid-late 20s, flirtatious and nice, even when he's being mean, tends to speak rapid-fire

SETTING

The park.

KEY

/ indicates overlapping dialogue as the next line begins
… indicates a struggle to articulate oneself, or a lost thought
— indicates a new, sudden thought, or jumping onto a better-worded sentence

Space between dialogue represents a silent and internal reaction, cautious thinking, a desire to speak before speaking, or a decision that some things are better left unsaid.

This play went to press before the end of rehearsals and may differ from the play as performed.

WARREN *waits in obscurity, under green foliage with his back to a large concrete wall.*

He clutches a tight fistful of twisted shopping bags: David Jones, JB Hi-Fi, Victoria's Basement et cetera. He stands awkwardly.

He stares at one particular entrance.

He rests his shopping bags on a nearby park bench.

Kneels into the bench with his back to the park. Puts his reading glasses on.

Holds his phone with both hands and privately searches his screen.

EDDEN *appears far off in the distance. He jogs along 'The Wall'. He darts across the street and paces along the perimeter of the park, glancing in distractedly.*

WARREN *notices* EDDEN. *Frowns toward him, strains. Takes his glasses off and stares pointedly.* EDDEN *notices* WARREN.

EDDEN *waves enthusiastically.*

WARREN *abandons his shopping bags on the park bench.*

Puts his hands in his front pockets.

EDDEN *is sweaty. He breathes heavily.*

WARREN: You been to a party, have you?
EDDEN: Hey?
WARREN: Fancy / shirt.
EDDEN: Aw yeah, nah nah.
WARREN: What?
EDDEN: Nah, I haven't.
 He tries to get his breath back.
 Fuck.
 Ran.
WARREN: Did you get stuck?
EDDEN: Yeah, sorry.
WARREN: No / you're right.
EDDEN: Did I leave you waiting?
WARREN: A bit. / You're alright.

EDDEN: Sorry.
WARREN:
EDDEN: Love a 'me day'.
WARREN: Hey?
> EDDEN *points at the shopping bags.*
> Oh sure, I was down at the Queen Elizabeth.
> It's a pretty building.
> Yeah, did a bit of a shop.
EDDEN: That's nice.
WARREN: It is, yeah.
> You wanna sit down for a moment?
> EDDEN *does.*
EDDEN: I'm super sweaty, hey.
> *He pulls at his jeans where they gather at the inside of his thighs.*
> Tight.
WARREN: I noticed they've got the new light rail—looks good. I haven't been down that way since they put it in.
EDDEN: Yeah, I / never go down th—
WARREN: You use it at all? It's paved along George Street now so …
> They used to have the monorail, this great big thing around Chinatown—Darling Harbour—they took that down. It was expensive.
> So … yeah so..
EDDEN: Mmm.
WARREN: What /about you, where are you based?
EDDEN: True true …
> I like your pics.
WARREN: Thanks, mate, yours too.
EDDEN: You look hairy.
> Do you have a hairy back?
> I've got a really hairy arse.
> Yeah, it's like, super hairy. Which sucks 'cause like I should be a twink.
WARREN:
EDDEN: Yeah, it's like—I should be a twink, hey.

WARREN: Doesn't matter.
EDDEN: My friend has an OnlyFans—and in all his videos his butt is jacked, but like he's actually not that peachy in real life—so it's like, 'How the fuck did you take that?'

I can never work out my angles. It's like try'na take a selfie—my hand can only reach so far.

WARREN *glances at someone or a group in the distance.*

It's outrageous.

EDDEN *follows* WARREN*'s gaze.*

They both stare at the group.

Are they looking at us funny?
WARREN: I think / they're fine.
EDDEN: They're alright, hey.
WARREN: You look ... familiar. How old are you?
EDDEN: I don't know you.

Are you from the country?
WARREN: ...
EDDEN: It's just the way you talk.
WARREN: Sure.
EDDEN: You look so donkey-dicked in your photos.
WARREN: Thank you.

I'm staying past the big Coca Cola.
EDDEN: Aww, okay.
WARREN: / ... I've got a room on Bayswater Road.

You do this often?
EDDEN: Yeah, I guess.
WARREN: I was / thinking you could come to—
EDDEN: Your dick's so fat, that's good. Do / you wanna go—
WARREN: My place is— / Oh, what?
EDDEN: Aw, you go. You go.
WARREN: I was gonna / say if you—
EDDEN: Are you straight?
WARREN:
EDDEN: No no, that's hot. That's totally hot.

You have a blank profile.
WARREN: I sent you my photos.

EDDEN: Oh god no! I love it, I love it ... I used to go to this beat—you know the toilets at the Domain Park? I'd go there all time 'cause—that's like all married guys—tradies, and like—there was always a lot of guys with crew cuts carrying Tarocash bags which is like definitely military, hey.

WARREN: The Domain? There's a navy base near there.

EDDEN: Yeah, right ... I'd just get down and blow dicks under the cubicle wall all day.

Like I wouldn't see their faces. Just random dicks. It was hot.

WARREN: You can come back to mine if you're discrete—we've got—a group of us have rooms booked out for work, so if you're happy to come in after me. If I walk in first.

EDDEN: Oh. You mean like sneak in?

Aw.

What about Bodyline?

WARREN: Say again?

EDDEN: Bodyline. It's like twenty-five dollars after four.

WARREN: Is that a club?

EDDEN: It's a sauna.

Are you alright?

WARREN: I'm fine thanks.

EDDEN: So do dunna go. Sorry—start again.

Do dunno go—fuck. I keep saying that, I'm like 'blurgh'!

He slows right down.

Do. You. Wanna. Go. To Bodyline? 'Cause it's just like literally—

He points.

You can't see—it's the other side of Oxford.

WARREN: You've already been today?

EDDEN *signals his 'entry band'.*

EDDEN: I found this one dom in there—like a dom daddy—but then I lost him—and like, everyone else was kind've shit ... I think just 'cause it was like middle of the day—week day.

Yeah, I found him later but he was sitting in the canteen ... it's like a time out zone—you can't have sex in there. He was on a computer doing emails or something. But it definitely picks up after eight if you're keen.

They've got this fuck room with windows.
You can get right up against the glass. The entire club pretty much ends up drooling like dogs ... it's very fucking hot.
You know how dogs do that when they wanna come inside? They're like ...
He imitates a little dog whimper.
WARREN: Just a sec, mate.
Come here a tick.
Look at me. Are you high?
EDDEN: No.
WARREN: Because I told you I don't do wyrd.
EDDEN: I'm not but. I'm not wryd. So.
WARREN: Just be honest, mate, you're behaving a little shady?
EDDEN: Oh my god, what?
You're shady as. Your profile is like empty.
WARREN: You don't look like your pictures at all if we're being honest.
EDDEN: Aww, okay.
WARREN: The filter you've put on everything
EDDEN: I don't do filters so—
WARREN: How old did you say you were?
EDDEN: Nineteen.
WARREN: Right.
EDDEN: Oh my god—which photo?
WARREN: Forget about it.
EDDEN: Nah, tell me the photo you're thinking of 'cause I'm like pretty sure they all look like me.
WARREN: All of them.
EDDEN: Oh my god, fuck you, you're shit.
WARREN: You should watch yourself, those places are crawling with gonorrhoea.
EDDEN: Um, okay, fuck you—they clean it heaps, like everything's plastic surfaces.
WARREN: You've already been with a couple of blokes today, have you?
EDDEN: Sorry—I don't get you—are you negging me right now?
WARREN: You use condoms?
EDDEN: ... I'm on PrEP.

EDDEN moves far away from WARREN.

WARREN: Well.
EDDEN: That's like so dickish. You don't know me.
WARREN: ... Oi.
Wait a sec.

> EDDEN *continues to move away—ignoring* WARREN. EDDEN *buries his head in his phone already returned to Grindr.*
>
> WARREN *catches up to him. They stop under a large tree at the top of the park.*

Straight back to Grindr.
EDDEN: Don't follow me.
WARREN: Sorry, mate, no I was—
EDDEN: You don't know me, get the fuck away from me.
WARREN: No, sor—

> EDDEN *makes such a big scene*—WARREN *tears away immediately and begins to walk in the other direction.*
>
> WARREN *stops for a moment. He hovers. His shoulders are tense.*
>
> *He lets out a frustrated sound.*

Oi.

> *He moves back toward* EDDEN.

Could I start again with this? I was a bit—
EDDEN:
WARREN: I'm only here this evening and then ahh ... off.
    The amount of men on here ... you'd think it'd be easy. I think there's one guy in this hotel I'm at but I can't see his face—I mean for all I know he's a colleague.
    Had a few no-shows last night.
EDDEN: Mm, that happens.
WARREN: I'd try and start a conversation—perfectly pleasant, get blocked. You boys just block people, don't you?
EDDEN: You shouldn't take it so personally.
WARREN: These two blokes, I was going to meet up with in Surry Hills—this couple—I didn't make it inside. I could see from their verandah—their windows were all blacked out with cardboard and masking tape.
    I'm sure you don't have / anything.
EDDEN: Gonorrhoea.

WARREN: You're very good looking.
EDDEN: Yes.
WARREN: What's your name?
EDDEN: / ... Edden— / I think this is like—
WARREN: Say again.
EDDEN: Edd. En.
WARREN: Edden.
EDDEN: Okay, cool.
WARREN: Maybe we can just chat first?
EDDEN: Oh my god, really?
    You should do eHarmony next time. Those people really enjoy talking and like—being frigid.
WARREN: Is there something wrong with talking first?
EDDEN: No, but you were literally saying the / filthiest fucking things and now you wanna chat—
WARREN: You blokes are in and out in a couple've minutes, then you're onto the next guy.
EDDEN: Okay.
WARREN: I've got a pack of beers in the fridge. I've got some craft beer.
EDDEN: Do you wanna see my dick?
WARREN: I do.
EDDEN: What else? Cum on my butthole.
WARREN: I could do that.
EDDEN:
WARREN: You could. Sit on my face.
EDDEN: Mmm, rub my pussy over you. Okay. Nice.
    Choke me? You wanna choke me?
WARREN: / ... I could
EDDEN: With your dick.
WARREN: Yes.
EDDEN: Would you reward me?
WARREN: Where'd you get that idea?
EDDEN: Why not?
    You could pay me.
WARREN: Too old, am I?
EDDEN: [*with a laugh*] No.
WARREN: Have to pay a fee? You charging these other blokes?

EDDEN: It's just hot. You wanna reward me?
I've got a really tight butt.
WARREN: ... I'd prefer not to.
EDDEN: Man, that's made me feel so bummed.
Why not?
I'm hot.
Man, I'm like—less than half your age.
WARREN: Thanks, mate, but I don't pay.
EDDEN: ...
What's this hotel like? You gotta spa bath?
WARREN: No, it's ... / shared bathrooms.
EDDEN: Oh my god, really?
WARREN: It's nice. There's a double bed. TV.
EDDEN: Ummm, yeaaah.
The OnlyFans guy I know—he just stayed in the Versace Hotel. He's just fucking away in this gigantic marble bathroom. And he put this post up where he like smashed a bottle of Bollinger—like just dropped it on the ground on purpose and he was like, 'Oops'—it's so cooked.
WARREN: I'm not following.
EDDEN: OnlyFans? It's like Instagram but people have to subscribe and pay to follow you, and you basically just send thirst trap videos or make actual porn.
I'm gonna start one. It's just a lot of content—like a lot of work.
WARREN: ... Can I show you something?

WARREN looks around gingerly.

He unlocks his phone. He searches his screen.

He sticks an earphone in. He offers the other earphone to EDDEN. EDDEN *takes it.*

EDDEN: Are you about to show me something fucked?

WARREN finds the video. Plays it.

Audio plays. It's hard to discern at first. Increasingly clear it's a video of WARREN *jacking off.*

WARREN stares at EDDEN *as he watches. He tries to hide a proud smile.*

Where's this?

WARREN: Cricket oval near our house.
EDDEN: What's that?
> WARREN *squints at the phone.*

Oh my god, it's a bin chicken!
Lol! It's like totally perving on you.
Oh, fuck, you're dirty.
> *They sit in stillness.* WARREN *holds the phone.* EDDEN *stares intently—amused.* WARREN *occasionally glances up to see if people are looking at them.*

WARREN: You'd like me to gag you?
EDDEN: With that? Oh my god.
> *A message appears on* WARREN*'s screen.* WARREN *flicks it away.*

Who's / that?
> WARREN *swipes the message away.*

Damn, look at you jizz.
> *A message appears again.*
> WARREN *tries to swipe it away.* EDDEN *snatches the phone.*

Who's Adam?
WARREN: Oi.
EDDEN: 'Are you in Syd yet?' Oh my god, who's Adam?
WARREN: He's no-one.
EDDEN: Can I see a—oh wow, yeah he's cute.
WARREN: Mate.
EDDEN: … Do you have any more videos? That was hot.
WARREN: I might have.
   What're you thinking then? You wanna come back?
EDDEN: I think you should invite that twink you're texting.
WARREN:
EDDEN: You're into younger, hey? Is that like a fetish?
WARREN: Mate. Can I have my son back?
   My phone! / My phone back.
EDDEN: Oh my god, he's your son.
WARREN: Alright—I'd prefer not to talk about family right now.
EDDEN: Does he know you're a little bit gay?

WARREN: No. That's not on. Are you gonna come back with me?
EDDEN: How old is he?
    You don't know?
WARREN: Nineteen. He's nineteen.
EDDEN: Oh shit.
    Oh wow. Do you think I look like him?
WARREN: / No.
EDDEN: I feel like we have similar bone structure.
WARREN: / No.
EDDEN: That is a bit fucked, isn't it? Is he fem?
WARREN: I wouldn't say that.
EDDEN: Okay, so he's a little bit fem.
WARREN: He lives in Sydney.
EDDEN: You worry about him?
WARREN: No—mate, you can stop asking questions about / Adam—I'm not up for talking about my son thanks. Really—that's—

WARREN's phone lights up. Siri: 'Calling Adam'.

EDDEN: / I meant like—meeting old sugar daddies in parks.

WARREN snatches his phone back.

The phone rings.

Being a cum / dump for—
VOICE: Hello.

They stare at the phone. EDDEN covers his mouth.

Hello, Dad.

WARREN holds the phone away from himself so he can read the screen properly.

He tears an earphone from EDDEN and moves a distance away.

EDDEN is left with one earphone.

WARREN: Mate.
VOICE: / What's up?
WARREN: Just calling to say I'm in Sydney—arrived safely. Day before yesterday actually—We were out in Paramatta to begin with though so—

VOICE: Nice. Where are you at the moment?
WARREN: We're ah—down at Opera Bar now. / Yeah, I think it's a bit of a work thing, mate.
VOICE: Oh, Amelia's probably working!
WARREN: Not Opera Bar!—I meant the other side, near the Passenger Terminal, / it's a work thing—
VOICE: Aw, I dunno.
WARREN: Is that your housemate Amelia? The blonde one.
VOICE: She's the one who came to schoolies?

> WARREN *turns to face* EDDEN *who is sniggering. He notices* EDDEN *is still listening through an earpiece.* WARREN *tries to tear it from him.*

WARREN: Yeah, okay. What's that?
VOICE: Dad—the girl who came with us to schoolies, you dropped us off.
> She was gonna join us later / if you—

WARREN: I think I'll have work to do tonight ... Hey, how're you going?
VOICE: Umm, I feel a bit shit. I'm just lying down.
WARREN: Oh right—that's no good.
VOICE: I think it's a gluten intolerance. I'm gonna try an Ayurvedic diet.
WARREN: What's that?
VOICE: Dad, I told you about Ayurveda. I wanted to take you while you're down—you can do yoga—but I was thinking you could get a consultation while you're here for your gout— / It's a healing—

> EDDEN *laughs.*

EDDEN: Oh my god.
VOICE: What ...?

> WARREN *rips the earphone from* EDDEN.

Did someone just laugh at me?
WARREN: No, mate—I'm just—we're shoulder to shoulder here, I just bumped into— [*Pretending to talk to someone*] S'cuse, sorry—thanks.
Bumped into a bloke. Look, it's getting a bit busy here so I might have to let you go.
VOICE: Okay ...
WARREN: You should take it easy then. Do you need some money?

VOICE: Maybe yeah.
WARREN: I'll have to—What?
VOICE: Maybe yeah.
WARREN: Oh, okay, well message me how much and I'll transfer you. It's been a while, I'll / have to catch you tomorrow—
VOICE: Yeah, it's been a minute— / Dad, also—Mum's asking for the receipts.
She's messaging the group chat.
WARREN: Alright.
VOICE: Did you sort out internet?
WARREN: / Yeaah—
VOICE: Let's just go to Broadway tomorrow—'cause I need to go to the Shaver Shop. We can grab breakfast at eight?
Shenkin in Newtown?
WARREN: What's it called?
VOICE: Shenkin / Kitchen. I'll text you.
WARREN: Shen.Kin?
VOICE: Also the gif you sent didn't make sense?
WARREN: What's that?
VOICE: The gif you put in the group chat.
WARREN: I thought it was funny.
VOICE: Yeah, it didn't make sense.
WARREN: Okay, mate.
I'll see you tomorrow.
Text it to me.
Okay. / 'Bye, mate.
VOICE: 'Bye, love y—

WARREN hangs up.

EDDEN: Oh my god. Do you feel like a dog?
I'm just teasing.
Yeah, I'll come back with you.

WARREN sits and recovers for a moment.

You okay?
WARREN: Mate.
EDDEN: I feel like we look the same.
WARREN: You don't.

EDDEN: I think it's hot.
WARREN:
EDDEN: I really like the Bel Ami porn where like there's the son and his hot friend is / over and they're making out.
WARREN: Come off it.
EDDEN: And the dad comes in. And the two of them start milking off the daddy, / looking up at him all doe-eyed.
WARREN: Enough!

He gets up and collects his shopping bags.

Mate, it's fucking disgusting.
EDDEN: Oh my god, I'm like joking.
Oh my god, you're so fucking serious. Chill out. Obviously that's like fucked—I'm just stirring.
WARREN:
EDDEN: Oh my god, are you actually pissed right now?
WARREN: What's your old man do, Edden?
EDDEN: I don't really know—something to do with WestPac maybe.
WARREN: How does he go with all this?
EDDEN: This what?
WARREN: This ... / affected way of speaking.
EDDEN: I did dancing when I was young, it's different.
Yeah, I did 'step ball change', jazz hands. Ballet. Wore a little ballet. Cup. Thing ...

Silence.

EDDEN *watches* WARREN *who is still clutching his shopping bags.*

WARREN:
EDDEN: I swear I will not mention him—also you should disable Siri.
WARREN: How do I do that?

EDDEN *takes* WARREN'*s phone. Disables Siri.*

This is a bit much for me.
EDDEN: Are you like flaking on me?
WARREN: You'll find someone.
EDDEN: Wait on ... / you're being a loser. Let's just chill here for a minute.
WARREN: I'm a little shaky. Give me a sec, Edden. I'm not sure.

EDDEN: Sure.

> *He produces a pack of canisters.*
>
> You want one?

WARREN: What are they?

EDDEN: It's so fine—these are super soft core.

WARREN:

EDDEN: It's basically just like vaping.

> EDDEN *places a canister into a cracker.*

WARREN: I need to find this … / receipt while I remember.

> WARREN *begins to sift through his shopping bags.*

EDDEN: Did you buy the wrong thing? She's gonna be angry.

WARREN: She might get angry. Adam's helping me tomorrow in case it's the wrong thing.

> EDDEN *tries to play a shy game of tootsies with* WARREN.
> WARREN *moves his feet.*

EDDEN: Are you like properly into her?
Sorry, off limits.

> WARREN *finds the receipt.*

WARREN: We've got this going round the clock. I can't keep up.

> *He holds it up to take a picture. Sends it.*

EDDEN: Is that like—family group chat?

WARREN: They'll probably tell me I got the wrong one. It was meant to be half price.

EDDEN: God, that's like a year's worth of shopping.
Are they Hush Puppies?

WARREN: What's that?

> WARREN *pulls the bag away from* EDDEN.

EDDEN: Hush Puppies are the devil. Just so you know.

> WARREN *locks his phone and looks at* EDDEN.
>
> EDDEN *offers* WARREN *a nang.*

You wanna try?
It lasts for like ten seconds … / Yeah, we could do it at your hotel?

WARREN: Are you losing the buzz?
EDDEN: I just had one beer today.

He offers the nang again.

Seriously, it's safe. You'll feel really sexy. You'll feel like a Ken doll.
WARREN: It looks like it'll knock you out, mate.

EDDEN *laughs. He slouches, pulls a balloon from his pocket and slips it over the canister.*

Do you study, Edden?
EDDEN: Yeah, I do art.
WARREN: You do art? Is that the degree, / is it?
EDDEN: I'm doing mix—mixed media—Media Arts.
WARREN: And what does that get you?
EDDEN: 'Scuse me?

WARREN *references the National Art School across the road.*

WARREN: You don't go over here, do you? Isn't this something?
EDDEN: It's the National.
WARREN: I thought so. You see them walking out of there with their … / hair.

I saw them all milling about this morning. Looks like a bit of fun.
EDDEN: I'd rather swallow my own arsehole, but yeah.

I go to UTS. I went to an open day here but. I didn't like, rate it.

Actually, I got this like really … / fucked feeling when we were doing the tour 'cause … / this whole area, it's called 'The Wall'. So it's like, built by convicts. There's convict markings all over it. 'Cause this was one've the—like first gaols.

It's totally haunted.
WARREN: It looks it. It's like something out of Harry Potter.
EDDEN: On the open day tour they were saying … there used to be this hangman. He had this massive scar down his face from an axe attack where some prisoner went ape shit and fully tried to attack him. Fucking iconic.

He actually lived in the park here. He had a little hut. And it was burned down by some little shits or something. He loses his mind and ends up in some mental asylum. But he hung heaps of people first! Like heaps.

It kinda makes you think like … are places like this fucking haunted or what? You know when places just keep attracting bad energy—it's like … That's definitely a thing.
 Are you gonna go find someone else? Or am I like the cutest boy on here?
  EDDEN *winks.* WARREN *laughs at this.*
WARREN: Maybe you should do history, Edden.
EDDEN: Nah, I'm gonna stick to art. I need to redo my Instagram but.
 They stare at The Wall in silence.
Actually I got followed by a car around here once.
 They are both staring at The Wall.
Right there, like literally—I was walking along … / this was years ago, I was like fifteen.
 The car was hovering just behind me—'cause I was walking through to Oxford. Maybe one a.m-ish.
WARREN: You didn't see his face?
EDDEN: Ah, yeaah, he didn't care! His window was fully down and he was just grinning at me.
 This massive fucking psycho grin.
 He'd drive past me, super slow, fully check me out, and then like, pull up just ahead of me. I'd get to about—there—and he'd ghost behind me again, overtake, pull in.
 It was a BMW. He had this umm car freshener tag thing—smelt like strawberry but like a super intense, sickly smell—'cause I ended up walking up to him and leaning in and being like, 'How much?'
WARREN: … And?
EDDEN: He said, 'Three hundred dollars'—I remember being like, 'That's decent.' I mean that's still decent.
 I guess I was looking pretty cute, I had these long socks on. I actually have no idea what he wanted to do though. He was such a loser, he was all stuttery and like so gross.
WARREN: Fifteen?
EDDEN: [*with a shrug*] I was seven when I came out.
WARREN: A lot of boys used to hang along here.
 This's where you'd get your male prostitutes hanging about.
EDDEN: Aww. Makes sense. Sex work.

WARREN: There used to be a … toilet block right there. It was a cruising spot.

A lot of young men heading in. Some of them'd come out with a broken nose.

Yeah, you'd get teenagers …

EDDEN: Hmm?

WARREN: … um.

You'd get … teenagers coming around when it turned dark. Basically picking fights.

EDDEN: Did you just go somewhere? Like mentally?

When was this?

WARREN: '83.

EDDEN: Mmm, okay, did somebody used to hang out here? Travel down to the big smoke for a bit of D.

WARREN: I lived here.

EDDEN: Are you for real?

WARREN: I am for real.

EDDEN: You must've hooked up heaps?

That would make you like forty percent gayer.

WARREN: Lived here for a few years when I was out of school.

Just there actually, Windsor Lodge. Wasn't / there very long—

EDDEN: Actually shush—I don't wanna know. It'll ruin it for me.

WARREN *watches* EDDEN *inhale a nang.*

WARREN: You're a bit of a party animal.

EDDEN *inhales and exhales, quietly. Meditatively. This takes some time.*

WARREN *is equal parts entranced and concerned.*

WARREN *looks around the park, a little paranoid of folk watching.*

EDDEN *releases the balloon. His arms drop by his side.*

EDDEN *collapses*—WARREN *tries to push him upright, but* EDDEN's *full body weight falls upon him.*

WARREN *tries to move* EDDEN *into an upright position.* EDDEN's *head flops back.*

EDDEN *begins to giggle.*

You right?

EDDEN: What is this right now? This is just so funny! Like whaaaat?

He's in disbelief. Having some kind of epiphany or a series.

EDDEN *giggles to himself.*

He looks at WARREN.

Why're you acting so precious?

WARREN: / You gave me a fright.

EDDEN: Chill out.

WARREN: What is this stuff?

EDDEN: It's so fine.

He rests in silence.

Wait. Did you say you used to live here?!

WARREN: Yeah, mate.

EDDEN: What, that's so random?

WARREN: What's this doing?

EDDEN: It's like massaging me.

Am I smiling?

WARREN: You are, looks like you're having a great time.

EDDEN: Is my face moving but?

He laughs hysterically.

Oh my god, my toes are like fully tingling.

He screams.

It's so weird, it's so ewww, but it's really nice at the same time. It's like ASMR.

WARREN: I don't know what you're talking about.

EDDEN: It just tingles everywhere. Like I can feel my pulse everywhere.

Yeah, I'm fully vibrating right now, hey. It's like I can feel my whole body—I feel so embodied and sexy and I feel like a big thumb. Like when you see someone who has a huge thick thumb—I just feel like I'm one really thick thumb on someone's hand. Like I'm growing outwards and getting really solid and thick.

It's like … I'm falling backwards into a tunnel—like I'm on a literal train just getting dragged backwards into a tunnel and I'm just looking out and it's getting fuzzier and further away and like—

Rolling onto his side, he looks at WARREN. *He squints his eyes and sprinkles his fingers at* WARREN.

Fuzz fuzz fuzz, that's what you are …

They sit in silence for some time. EDDEN*'s eyes glaze.*

EDDEN *reaches for* WARREN*'s dick.*

Yes, okay, I need to see your dick now.

Seriously—no seriously, let me. Please. Honestly, like no-one's watching.

Just flick it out. Flick it.

WARREN: Mate, get a handle on yourself. Get your hands off me.

EDDEN: Excuse me, do you wanna fuck me? I'm so fucking horny now. Honestly, you would be so lucky—

WARREN: You're out of control.

EDDEN: Naah.

WARREN *removes* EDDEN*'s hands, holds his wrists together.*

WARREN: Edden, listen to me—you're behaving like a fucking child.

EDDEN: You're a pussy.

WARREN: I don't do this, mate.

EDDEN: Bullshit. I bet you take amyl?

WARREN: I don't. Don't raise your voice.

EDDEN: I knew this dude who took amyl through one of those those old World War Two pilot masks. It felt like I was getting fucked by Bane—you know that guy from *Batman*.

WARREN:

EDDEN: He'd lie there while I blew him. And then he'd push my head into the mattress and fuck me—with this huge amyl mask on.

Does your wife know you take / amyl?

WARREN: You're completely out of it, aren't you?

EDDEN: Fuck you. Out've what?

WARREN *looks around the park.*

WARREN: You're not shy.

EDDEN: Were you expecting me to be shy? You were hoping I'd be a tiny, tiny, little shy boy.

He starts to touch himself.

He's probably on Grindr.
Do you think he's a twink or an otter?
Adam.
Does that touch a nerve? Talking about / your son?
WARREN: You know it does.
Are you doing this right here, / are you?
EDDEN: Is he twink or otter? Or is he like—ripped?
WARREN: You look like you're completely out of it.
EDDEN: I'm try'na get you hard. Come on.
No-one's even looking at us.

> WARREN *hesitates a moment.*
>
> *He puts his hand on* EDDEN's *jaws.* EDDEN *lets him. He sticks his thumb in* EDDEN's *mouth.*

WARREN: You like a belly?
EDDEN: I love a belly.

> WARREN *pushes his hand into* EDDEN's *pants.*
>
> WARREN *tries to jack* EDDEN *off.* EDDEN *remains limp.*
>
> WARREN *tries a little more vigorously.*

God, this is fucking sad ...
Say something fucked. Actually, just slap me.
WARREN: Don't go drawing attention.
EDDEN: Oh my god, just call me a little bitch please.
WARREN: Shhh. Keep your / voice d—
EDDEN: Let's get out of this fucking park.

> WARREN *leans in to kiss* EDDEN. EDDEN *leans back onto the shopping bags.*

Can you say something fucked—fuck—what the fuck am lying on?
WARREN: It's the—
EDDEN: Oh my god, is that the Hush Puppies? / Christ.
WARREN: Here.

> WARREN *tries to move the Hush Puppies.*

EDDEN: Oh my god, Jesus.

> *He sits up.*

Just wait.

WARREN: You alright?
EDDEN: My head's spinning
WARREN: You can come back to mine. We'll get you / some water.
EDDEN: No. No, I'm not feeling this.
    I'm not feeling it.
    God, what the fuck am I doing?

    WARREN*'s phone starts ringing.* WARREN *puts it on vibrate.*

    EDDEN *buries his head in his hands.*

WARREN: They're for my wife. She works on her feet all day.
EDDEN: …
WARREN: That balloon's really messed you up.
EDDEN: It's not the balloon.
WARREN:
EDDEN: … Can you please undo your top button?
WARREN: Are you alright, mate?
EDDEN: I just need to lie down for a sec.

    WARREN *stares at* EDDEN.

WARREN: I've got another video I can show you—with a guy from work?
EDDEN:
WARREN: He was a—an out gay. A few years ago. He's up at Broken Hill now.
    We did some … / good stuff
EDDEN: I need to get out of this park.
    I can't believe I was just begging you.

    He holds his head.

I just get this … dissociation sometimes, where I feel like—distant from myself, and I'm watching myself and I'm like, 'What am I doing here?'
WARREN: You don't think it's the—thing you took?
EDDEN: Sorry, do you have a water bottle in there?

    They sit in silence a moment.

    EDDEN *sits up. He produces another nang.*

WARREN: You don't think you should slow down.
EDDEN: Nah, sometimes—it's fine, I get anxious but then I do a few more and it's good.

He exhales deeply.

Oh my god, like I have assignments to do.

I think I need some G.

WARREN: Why don't you come back to mine and do this?

EDDEN: Nah, man.

WARREN: This's a bit've a dodgy area …

EDDEN: Are you hoping I'll pass out on your lounge?

WARREN: No.

EDDEN: Some guys prefer that.

Having a little limp boy in their apartment.

WARREN: No. No no.

EDDEN: Nah, I don't wanna hook up with you. I feel like I just need to chill out.

You can go, man.

WARREN: Aright.

I used to live here, that's all. Up that way. I know it's a—it can be a dangerous area. That's where I'm coming from.

EDDEN: Thank you.

WARREN: So you're just going to lay here? Pass out again?

EDDEN: Pretty much.

Nice to meet you, though. Sorry for being so random.

WARREN *stares at his phone, and flicks desperately.*

WARREN: I'll try and find this other video for you.

EDDEN: Just send it to me on Grindr—

WARREN: It doesn't look like you can send video files.

Come back to mine and have a lie down.

EDDEN: I need to move my legs.

WARREN: I'll walk you to the … / the …

WARREN *is stuck in his phone.*

EDDEN: I need to move my legs.

WARREN: Here. You're on Whatsapp, aren't you?

/ We don't have to.

EDDEN: Why? Are you gonna hit me up when you're in town again?

WARREN: You don't have to reply.

This's been nice, though. Talking.

Block me if you're not into it.

EDDEN: ... I got Whatsapp.

    EDDEN *takes* WARREN*'s phone, types his number in.*

WARREN: Don't message me.
EDDEN: Yeah yeah.
WARREN: I'll message you. It's better.

    EDDEN *hands the phone back.*

I'll walk you to this sauna.
EDDEN: I'm actually / fine.
WARREN: No, I'll show you this on the way.
EDDEN: I can take myself there.

    EDDEN *makes to walk away.*

    WARREN *watches him go ...*

    WARREN *unlocks his phone, sends a message.*

WARREN: Oi, Edden!
    Check your phone.

    EDDEN *looks down at his phone. Hovers for a moment.*

Watch it here, mate.
EDDEN: / It's okay.
WARREN: Watch it here so I can see your reaction.

    WARREN *chuckles.*

    He stares after EDDEN.

EDDEN: Is this you being a dirty fucker?
WARREN:

    WARREN *just smiles.*

EDDEN: Thanks, yeah. Yeah, sorry about that—it was weird.
    Okay.

    He hovers.

I might just get walking now.
WARREN: Just a sec, mate. Watch it here.

    EDDEN *hovers over his screen.*

    WARREN *looks at* EDDEN *with an open gaped smile. He waits for* EDDEN*'s reaction.*

It come through yet?
EDDEN: …
WARREN: Oh well.

> WARREN *picks up his shopping bags but he doesn't move—he stares after* EDDEN *waiting for a reaction.*
>
> WARREN *puts his shopping bags on the ground between his legs. Grabs his phone. Unlocks it.*
>
> *Stares at the screen.*

EDDEN: Do you have Bluetooth? You can Bluetooth it.

> WARREN *deflates. His hand rises to his mouth or forehead.*
>
> EDDEN *moves back toward him.*

Give us a look.
WARREN: Fucking hell.
EDDEN:
WARREN: Can I retrieve that?

> EDDEN *takes* WARREN*'s phone. Stares at the screen.*

EDDEN: I don't think so.
Oh my god. Oh shit. Wait, this's the group chat?

> *He starts laughing. He presses 'play'. For the briefest second the sound of* WARREN *fucking some other man.*

Oh my god.
No-one's writing back but.
WARREN: I can't retrieve it?
EDDEN: I don't think so but it's—

> *He covers his mouth in disbelief.*
>
> *He composes himself.*

We could maybe google if there's a way.
That's like definitely more daddy-ish. More where I was leaning.

> WARREN *snatches his phone back, chucks it on the park bench but remains standing.*

Don't forget your bags.

> EDDEN *picks them up, holds them out for* WARREN.

WARREN: Yeah, can you google it, mate?

EDDEN *pulls out his phone. Searches.*

EDDEN: Umm ... Jesus, this is stressful. Um.
Have they seen it?

WARREN *grabs his phone. His hand tremors. He can't type.*

[*Reading off the phone*] 'For any message that you send, you'll be able to see a message info screen, displaying the details of when your message was delivered, read, or played by the recipient. To see the message info screen: Open an individual or group chat. Tap and hold your sent message.'

He takes the phone from WARREN.

WARREN *clutches himself.*

I can't believe this is actually happening, hey.

WARREN *death-stares* EDDEN.

Maybe you should call them and tell them not to / look at it—
WARREN: Call all six of them.
My daughter-in-law's on there.
EDDEN: You're shaking.

WARREN *sinks into the park bench.* EDDEN *stands awkwardly. Taps his fingers along the wood of the bench impatiently while he thinks.* WARREN *puts a hand on him to stop him from tapping.*

I don't think there's much you can do.
Unless you call just—like the more important person and just tell them.
No-one's seen it yet—oh, wait. Oh. Yeah, okay.
WARREN: Who's seen it?
EDDEN: Who's Tabby?
WARREN: Tabitha. That's my wife.
Has Adam seen it?
EDDEN: Um ... not yet.

WARREN *begins to tremble.*

WARREN *begins to cry.*

Do you think they already know?

WARREN *composes himself.*

His phone begins to vibrate on silent.

It stops.

WARREN*'s phone begins to vibrate again, longer. Ceaselessly.*

She's calling you.

EDDEN *puts the phone on mute.*

WARREN *grabs the phone from* EDDEN *and chucks it into the green foliage.*

He sits down.

WARREN *gets up to go and find the phone.* EDDEN *grabs him. Lets go immediately.*

Sorry.

They stand in silence a moment.

WARREN:
EDDEN: … What're you gonna do?
WARREN: I don't know. Call my son maybe. This'll kill him.
EDDEN: No, he'll be fine.
WARREN: This'll kill him.
EDDEN: Okay … ummm …

I had a panic attack once. At this festival … Alt-J were playing and I'd just taken this random synthetic drug that we'd got from some TSG store—Anyway this girl had a gigantic watermelon and she was like, 'Lay down, let me roll this watermelon over you'. She rolled it over my body and the weight of it—and the coolness of it was. Really helpful.

WARREN: You can go, mate.

Really. I'll be fine. Off you go please.

EDDEN *remains.*

EDDEN: Did you like, go to Catholic school? They beat the gay away?
WARREN: Baptist.
EDDEN: Baptist!

Yeaah, they're like total dogs, hey.

WARREN:
EDDEN: I went to a—random Catholic school.

They wouldn't let us play Elton John.

But they did let us play Queen which is …
What's your name?
WARREN: …
EDDEN: Oh my god. You can stalk my Facebook. I swear to god I'm pretty sure we don't have any mutual friends—you're like so old.
WARREN: Warren.
EDDEN: What? / Warren.
WARREN: Warren.
EDDEN: This'll be fine! Seriously. It's fucked up but this is just one of those really devastating times in a family. But some people get over it.

Like my friend Amy—she found out her dad had like, a secret family in Ubud.

It was so fucked. Her half sisters went fucking psycho 'cause they were totally trying to steal her life … but her dad and mum … Aw actually, that didn't go so well 'cause he'd been funnelling money from the family business that he and the mum had built from the ground up … but they still speak.
WARREN:
EDDEN: You know … you could … get the uniform around here—black gym clothes—little shorts—find some hot guy who owns a grocery store in Potts Point and like fully like wake up every day with him and like. Finger him.
WARREN: That's not what I want, mate. I love Tabitha.
EDDEN: Yeah, okay.

No, I believe you—you think she's hot …?
WARREN: She is hot. She's great—we have great sex. We go to the Gordon every Thursday—we listen to live music. I'm … I've got no interest in changing things.
EDDEN: Oh okay, that's total bullshit.

Are you kidding? Man, you're gay.
WARREN: Honestly, shut up please.
EDDEN: You're like in denial.
WARREN: You're not—
EDDEN: Not what? Are you gonna finish that?
WARREN: You don't know what you're talking about.

Mate—how long have you been with someone?
EDDEN: I just want you to be happy and be like / honest about that—

WARREN: Are you happy? On your Instagram all day. / Checking all your likes—How old are you?
EDDEN: I delete my Instagram all the time!
WARREN: How old are you?
EDDEN: Excuse me.
WARREN: You're not nineteen.
EDDEN: Um, fuck you, yeah I am.
WARREN: Mate, how many filters did you put on those pictures?
EDDEN: I don't need filters. That's like—filters aren't a thing anymore, that's like so mid-2000s, you shit head.
WARREN: Calm down.
EDDEN: That's really offensive, how old do you think I am?
WARREN: Don't worry, mate.
EDDEN: No, how—
WARREN: Edden, please.

They sit in silence.

WARREN *stares at his hand, it's tremoring like crazy.*

EDDEN: Do you want me to go find you a watermelon?
WARREN: Can you just sit with me?

EDDEN *holds* WARREN's *hand.*

Silence.

Let's do one of those …
EDDEN: What, a nang?
WARREN: Come on. Yes, come on.

WARREN *looks at his own fingers. They tremble still.*

EDDEN *makes up another nang.*

EDDEN: … It's like a light buzz, it's nice.
How's your heart?
WARREN: Still going.

WARREN *waits.* EDDEN *takes out the equipment.*

WARREN *sits solemnly.*

EDDEN *fills a balloon.* WARREN *tries to take it—his hands shake so he lets go.*

EDDEN *hands him the balloon.* WARREN *fumbles with his fingers but manages.*

EDDEN *silently coaches the balloon to* WARREN*'s mouth.*

WARREN *inhales and exhales.*

WARREN *inhales and exhales, quietly. Meditatively. Dropping into himself.*

WARREN *releases the balloon. His arms drop by his side.*

The sound of the nang echoes in WARREN*'s ears and he plummet backwards into some deep and distant place.*

EDDEN *follows closely behind him, inhaling his own nang.*

They are very chill.

EDDEN: When did it turn dark?
 … I wonder if old Alexander Green comes out at night to hang people.

WARREN: The hangman?

EDDEN: Yeah, I wonder if anyone's ever seen him. I'm gonna google that.
 Just running around with a noose or something.

WARREN *chuckles.*

WARREN: Well, you'd like that, wouldn't you? You're into getting choked.

EDDEN *bursts into laughter.*

EDDEN: Oh my god, that's fucking funny. Maybe he's my ultimate dom. Lol.
 Will you still stay here tonight?

WARREN: Well, yes. I was meant to be seeing my son in the morning. And then back home.
 I'm from Goulburn.

EDDEN: My grandparents live out there.
 You've got like two McDonald's on either side of the road. It's so dumb.

WARREN: It's for people coming both sides of the highway, / if they're passing through

EDDEN: I get that.
 Are there no other guys in Goulburn?

WARREN: In Crookwell. They're into chem sex.

EDDEN: Where's Cowra?
WARREN: That's too far. We went out that way for a trampoline. That's miles away.
EDDEN: How long've you been on Grindr?
WARREN: I don't know, mate. Deleted it that many times.
EDDEN: Whenever I go out somewhere rural it's just like a million blank profiles, it's so shit. And the closest guy is like twenty k's away.
I almost feel like it's like better to do old school—like Craigslist. Like a classifieds ad.

WARREN *laughs at this.*

WARREN *breathes deeply.*

WARREN: I had a … Chatroulette account for a while. It's an / adult cam site account.
EDDEN: Oh wow, yeah, that's like so real.
WARREN: I had—some. Stupid name. And when they were asleep … Because my office at home is right down the hall. I'd get up and, I can't believe I'm telling you this.

I'd face the—face the laptop to the door. I'd have my stack of—reports to do—for work. I'd put my reading glasses on …

All of these boys … / [*He motions his hand.*] All these channels. I actually started—ah, paying for one of them. This boy in … Canada. He was always happy to chat back. And so I'd—put some tokens on his show. Ask for things. Just a. To hear him say my name or something.

Then I'd go back to bed. I seriously wouldn't think about it again. I mean, you do it all late at night—this stuff—and you can kind've convince yourself you're not doing it.

Anyway I stopped doing it. Adam got to an age … I'd get up at night and my laptop'd be missing—he'd gotten up before me, snuck into his room with it. I know he was watching porn because all my history was cleared.

It all got a bit much—suddenly he's the same age as these boys … That got a little. Confronting.

I've got other sons. But … I mean we're closer so it's / strange.
EDDEN: Feels perverse …?
WARREN: Strange I think.

EDDEN: I used to be on some of those sites. They say it's like gambling—the design, with the tokens stacking up. You slide forward so all these faceless accounts can see your cunt and the tokens just stack up.

... Did you feel lucky when I replied to your messages?
WARREN: You wrote to me.

You sent me a whole lot of pictures of your arse, mate.
EDDEN: ...

There's this guy at my work ... and he's my age and it's. Weird.

I should be so keen on him. He's properly wholesome. Like he took me on this night swim once, and he's got a whippet ...
WARREN: You'll find someone who makes you tick, mate.
EDDEN: ...

There's an alcohol and ... drug service here. Yeah, I went in a year ago ... It's fun for me now, it's not like a problem—but when I went in at that time it was like ... a problem. And I remember thinking—I'm gonna get out of here and go find a therapist. Get a mental health plan sorted. Get a boyfriend.

And I was meant to go see this National Theatre Live thing with him ... This is three days ago but I ended up going to this warehouse in Sydenham ... There was this guy there ... I dunno. His teeth were like—mank ...

We went into this room—behind all of these storage boxes. He gives me pink undies. He says they're his girlfriend's. There is no girlfriend ... I get a hundred dollars and a hit of G.

And I went to a sauna afterwards. And—yeah, I didn't go home. Now I'm here.
WARREN: Three days ...?
EDDEN: Mhm.

Umm.

I'm twenty-four.

I'm twenty-four. I just say I'm nineteen 'cause that's what doms are into.

It's fucked.
WARREN: It is actually, yes.

Are they your photos?
EDDEN: They're my photos—they're just like, from a few years ago.

I think I ... / don't look as hot maybe.

WARREN: You're fine, mate.

EDDEN: Nah, I had like, so many more followers then.

It's so depressing. I've started my Instagram over like that many times.

WARREN: Edden.

EDDEN: Mmm.

WARREN: Edden.

EDDEN: What?

WARREN: I told you I used to live at Windsor Lodge … / it's up that street over there.

There used to be … up by that wall—they had the toilet block.

The Green Park toilets. They got knocked down.

EDDEN: You said this. Maybe just be chill now.

WARREN: Well, there was this—young bloke who used to live around here. We were the same age at that time. So seventeen, eighteen. I haven't thought about him in forever. But um … when I saw you. Earlier. You know, I thought you looked familiar … I couldn't work it out.

You look like a dead ringer. Edden.

He was handsome. He used to wear a lot of product in his hair. Always at the pub, always with a group of friends. Loud. And. I'd met him in the toilets which used to be here … we would pass each other—we never—interacted.

But …

I found him. I found his body. In the toilets …

It's very odd being back here …

I used to go after ten in the evening. Walk down from my place. It was a lot quieter on Thursdays.

And this night. He was curled up in a cubicle. Pushed into a cubicle and. Covered in newspaper.

EDDEN:

WARREN *blindly reaches for* EDDEN*'s hand. He finds it.*

WARREN: … Is my hand too sweaty?

He lets go. EDDEN *takes his own hand back.*

Someone put a sheet of newspaper over his face. It was like they'd attacked him but—it was like they'd wrapped him in a blanket afterwards, it seemed gentle.

EDDEN: [*with a laugh*] Sorry. Oh my god—I'm not laughing at this. I'm not.

He grabs his head with both hands and tries to calm down.

Aw fuck. This is so fucking weird.

I've been in this park way too long.

They sit in silence.

WARREN: I don't mean to scare you.

EDDEN: It's not scary.

WARREN: It is scary.

Hmm.

I didn't even think when I was waiting for you—when you dropped the pin on the map I thought … 'Oh, that's the park.' But. I didn't really think.

You have his hair.

EDDEN: You need to see a psych.

…

Did you report it?

WARREN:

EDDEN: Did you report it?

Oh my god, are you fucking kidding me?

WARREN *sits in an uncomfortable silence.*

WARREN *observes his hand again. No longer tremoring.*

WARREN: It's right, what you said. About these places being haunted.

EDDEN: I have to go.

WARREN: I'd prefer you don't go right now.

EDDEN: I totally get that but—I'm anxious at the best of times. Like I know a decent person would sit with you right now but I can't.

EDDEN *gets up, shakes the juju off.*

He turns and stares at WARREN *who stares at his blank phone screen.*

WARREN: You don't want to stay with me?

EDDEN: No.

WARREN: You're the first person I've told.

EDDEN: … Alright.

Maybe you should go do a—confessional or something …

EDDEN *paces. Makes to walk away.*

WARREN: Come back to mine, I'll get us some food. You hungry? Edden?

Come on, mate.

EDDEN: I'm pretty happy to go.

WARREN: You wanna massage or something?

EDDEN *laughs at this.*

Hey, oi.

I'll pay you.

EDDEN *stops.*

I'd prefer not to be alone right now.

Edden, you want me to buy you something? How much does a bag cost?

EDDEN: A bag of what?

WARREN: Here you go. I'll get you whatever you want ... / I don't care.

EDDEN: Fuck you.

WARREN: Just tell me what you want.

EDDEN: Seriously?

WARREN: Yeah, mate.

EDDEN: Um.

WARREN: You wanna just stay up and fuck all night. Take some—what is it?

EDDEN: G?

WARREN:

EDDEN *hesitates.*

EDDEN: I'm gonna go that way, Warren.

WARREN: Right.

EDDEN: Right.

EDDEN *doesn't move.*

WARREN: ...

I don't want to be alone, mate, that's all.

EDDEN: ... Umm.

Oh, shit.

No.

WARREN: Fine.

EDDEN: You know I used to be on some of those sites.
That boy lets you pay him tokens 'cause it's hot.
It's hot when someone wants your arse that much.
WARREN: Okay.
EDDEN: When the tokens are stacking up and there are like a hundred faceless accounts watching ... And you slide forward so they can all see your cunt and the tokens just like stack up.

EDDEN starts to move away.

WARREN: Where're you going?
... Edden, come on—
EDDEN: I dunno. Like I wanna say home, but I won't.
WARREN: Okay.
EDDEN: Okay.

EDDEN hesitates. He leaves.

WARREN stares at this phone. He stands up, moves a short distance across the park. He stares at the blank screen. He turns his phone on. The screen illuminates his face.

He walks until he disappears.

THE END

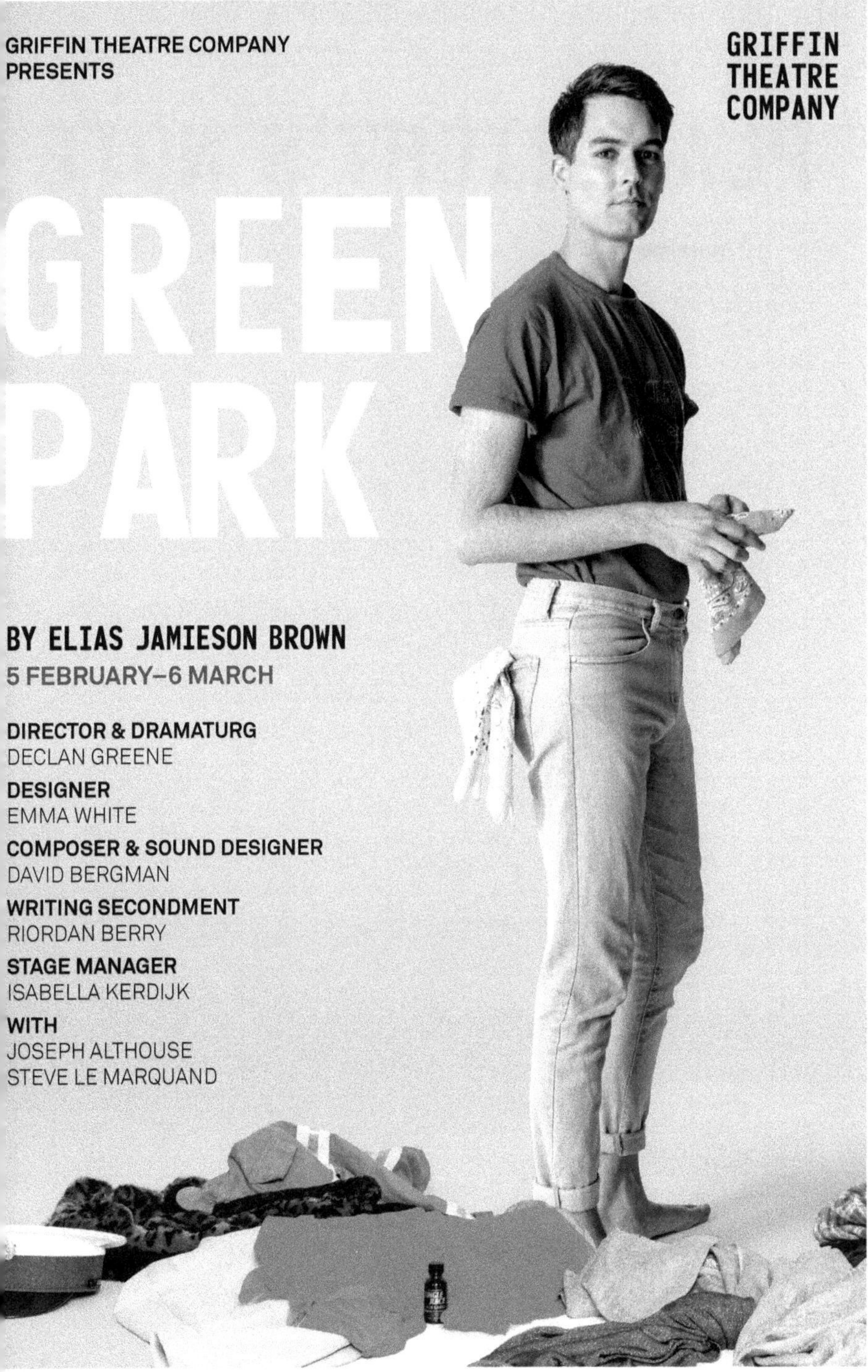

GRIFFIN THEATRE COMPANY PRESENTS

GRIFFIN THEATRE COMPANY

GREEN PARK

BY ELIAS JAMIESON BROWN
5 FEBRUARY–6 MARCH

DIRECTOR & DRAMATURG
DECLAN GREENE

DESIGNER
EMMA WHITE

COMPOSER & SOUND DESIGNER
DAVID BERGMAN

WRITING SECONDMENT
RIORDAN BERRY

STAGE MANAGER
ISABELLA KERDIJK

WITH
JOSEPH ALTHOUSE
STEVE LE MARQUAND

Supported by
Government partners

Griffin acknowledges the generosity of the Seaborn, Broughton & Walford Foundation in allowing it the use of the SBW Stables Theatre rent free, less outgoings, since 1986.

PLAYWRIGHT'S NOTE

I first presented *Green Park* at Melbourne Theatre Company for their Cybec Electric program. As the writing developed, a few people suggested I rename the play and set it in Victoria. They wanted it to be relevant to local audiences.

I was stubbornly protective but couldn't articulate why I felt this park was essential as the dramatic backdrop to Edden and Warren's story. Interviews with Queers and research spirals revealed an endlessly fascinating history. It's difficult now to think of another setting, fictional or existing, that lends itself to such loaded symbolism.

I already knew Green Park as the site of the Gay and Lesbian Holocaust Memorial, and the first AIDS Memorial Candlelight Rally. I learned it's the site where the Sisters of Perpetual Indulgence gathered in 1984 to commemorate the men's public toilet after it was demolished—because it was operating as a kind of all-hours sex haunt.

In developing this play, we often spoke about the ghosts and tragedy that surround Warren and Edden; their meeting place is wedged between Old Darlinghurst Gaol, the Holocaust Museum and St Vincent's Hospital, which was one of the first health care facilities in Australia to treat AIDS patients.

In the past, it was a meeting place for closeted men and sex workers at a time when it was criminal to practise homosexuality. Now it continues as a meeting place for the homeless.

It's as though it's always been a kind of purgatory for people who feel rejected by society.

Rewriting this play to be performed as a site-specific work took a lot more time and development than Declan and I anticipated. But the nerd in me adores how firmly rooted this play is to its location, and I hope the audience leaves with an affection for the real Green Park.

I will be eternally grateful to Declan and the Griffin team for supporting this work through its many iterations and of course, for premiering my first mainstage play.

Elias Jamieson Brown

DIRECTOR'S NOTE

In the depths of Sydney's first COVID-19 lockdown, I was having a socially-distanced coffee with Simon Burke somewhere in Kings Cross. At this time, in April 2020, performing indoors in a conventional theatre seemed a million years away, so I was trying to come up with an idea for a show that Griffin could stage outdoors. After Simon had talked me down from some truly woeful ideas, we moved on, and I started telling him about the young writer Elias Jamieson Brown, and a brilliant play he'd written that touched on the complex history of Darlinghurst's Green Park. Simon offered: *'Could you do it in the real Green Park?'* I told him no—Elias's play was set in a Darlinghurst apartment. *'...But could you do it in the real Green Park?'*

I called Elias and suggested it would be very easy to relocate the setting of his play, requiring minimal interference to his script.

Six months later he had written a completely new play.

I can't say I don't feel bad for that other version of *Green Park*. It was a great play: just as funny and profound as all of Elias's work. But I'm also glad *Green Park* was rewritten. Not just because of its potential as a site-specific show, but because Elias had started writing *Green Park* in 2018, and now in 2021, the gay world which that early draft reflected has changed massively.

Griffin has a long and great history of staging works about contemporary gay experience. From the landmark devised work *Soft Targets*, to Tommy Murphy's *Strangers in Between*, to Alana Valentine's *Ladies Day*. But these were all written before the legalisation of same-sex marriage in Australia. The post-Marriage Equality gay world is quite a new place, and the real Green Park stands as an increasingly potent metaphor for it.

In Elias's play, Edden and Warren enter this park as two men who should, in 2021, be 'fine'. Edden is a brashly queer member of Gen Z. Warren is a maybe-straight-maybe-bi Gen X-er. Both of them are same-sex-attracted, both of them live in a country where such relationships are broadly accepted.

But neither Warren nor Edden are, in fact, 'fine'. They arrive in the park looking for quick sex, and find themselves tangled in decades of trauma. On one side: the ghost of a toilet block where men would meet for anonymous sex under threat of bashing. On the other side: a hospital where many of those same men died of AIDS. A decades-long history of queer lust, repression, violence—now half-forgotten beneath a veneer of polite gay gentrification. A Fitness First hasn't been built over it yet. But at some point it probably will be.

As a director, it is always a privilege to direct a premiere of a new work, but I am doubly grateful for the opportunity to also work with Elias as Dramaturg of his play. Whatever we define as 'truth' in 2021, he has an innate and precious gift for it—bringing Warren and Edden to life in all their glorious mess with the tiniest, most striking details. Even in 2021, it is still rare to see queer characters of this depth and complexity on the Australian stage.

…Or patch of grass, as it were.

Declan Greene

BIOGRAPHIES

ELIAS JAMIESON BROWN
PLAYWRIGHT

Elias is a Master of Writing for Performance graduate from Victorian College of the Arts (2017). He is a recipient of the Jim Marks Scholarship from the University of Melbourne. His work has been supported by the Playking Foundation, Creative Victoria's VicArts Grant, and Critical Mass at Brunswick Mechanics Institute. He has presented new writing at MTC's Cybec Electric, Red Stitch Actors' Theatre's *PLAYlist*, for Australian Theatre for Young People (ATYP), Periscope Productions, Apocalypse Theatre, and the Old 505 Theatre. He has been shortlisted for the Next Stage Residency at MTC, the National Script Workshop at Playwriting Australia, and the Silver Gull Playwriting Award. He is an alumnus of the Fresh Ink National Mentorship program and the National Studio at ATYP.

Elias directed two sold-out seasons of Chloe Moss's *This Wide Night* at The Burrow, Fitzroy, and executive produced and co-wrote the feature film *Ambrosia*, winner of the Special Jury Prize at the Gulf of Naples Independent Film Festival and Best Cinematography at the Harrisburg-Hershey Film Festival.

DECLAN GREENE
DIRECTOR & DRAMATURG

Declan is the Artistic Director of Griffin Theatre Company, and works as a playwright, dramaturg and director. As a director, his credits include: for Malthouse Theatre: *Wake in Fright*; for Malthouse Theatre and Sydney Theatre Company: *Blackie Blackie Brown*; for Sydney Theatre Company: *Hamlet: Prince of Skidmark*; for ZLMD Shakespeare Company: *Conviction*. As a playwright, his work includes *Eight Gigabytes of Hardcore Pornography*, *The Homosexuals, or 'Faggots'*, *Melancholia*, *Moth*, and *Pompeii L.A.* Declan co-founded queer experimental theatre company Sisters Grimm with Ash Flanders in 2006, and has directed and co-created all their productions to date, including: for Griffin Independent and Theatre Works: *Summertime in the Garden of Eden*; for Malthouse Theatre and Sydney Theatre Company: *Calpurnia Descending*; for Melbourne Theatre Company: *Lilith: The Jungle Girl*; and for Sydney Theatre Company: *Little Mercy*. He was previously Resident Artist at Malthouse Theatre.

EMMA WHITE
DESIGNER

Emma White is a set and costume designer for stage and screen. Emma is a graduate of NIDA's MFA Design course and has a BFA in Sculpture from UNSW Art and Design. In 2019, Emma was nominated for an APDG Award for Best Emerging Designer for Live Performance and was selected for APDG's Mentor program. Since graduating, Emma has worked regularly as a design assistant to Elizabeth Gadsby alongside working in the costume department at Belvoir St Theatre. Emma's theatre credits include: as Set and Costume Designer: for Belvoir 25A: *Kasama Kita*; for Bondi Feast: *The Knife*; for The Blue Room Theatre/Sotto: *You've Got Mail*; for Milk Crate Theatre: *Natural Order*; for National Theatre of Parramatta/Sydney Festival: *Boom*; for NIDA: *Stay Happy Keep Smiling*, *Venus in Fur*; for the Old 505: *Homesick*; for the Old 505/Sotto: *Safe*; for Q Theatre: *Daisy Moon Was Born This Way*; for Red Line Productions at the Old Fitz: *Chorus*; as Associate Designer: for Hayes Theatre Co.: *American Psycho*; for Sport for Jove: *A Misdummer Night's Dream*, *The Tempest*; as Assistant Designer: for National Theatre (UK): *Nine Night*; for Shakespeare's Globe: *Richard II*; and for Sydney Theatre Company: *Lord of the Flies*.

DAVID BERGMAN
COMPOSER & SOUND DESIGNER

David is a composer, sound and video designer and has been based in Sydney for over 10 years. His recent work includes: as Composer & Sound Designer: for Griffin: *First Love is the Revolution*, *Superheroes*; for Darlinghurst Theatre Company: *Maggie Stone*; for NIDA: *Another Country*, *SALEM*; for Seymour Centre: *Made to Measure*; as Sound and Video Designer: for Soft Tread Enterprises: *The Gospel According to Paul*; for Sydney Theatre Company: *A Cheery Soul*, *The Wharf Revue* (2009-2019); as Sound Designer: for ATYP: *Spring Awakening*; for Hayes Theatre Company: *Catch Me If You Can*, *The Rise and Disguise of Elizabeth R*; for Monkey Baa: *Josephine Wants to Dance*; as Co-Sound Designer: for Belvoir: *Packer and Sons*; as Video Designer: for Bangarra: *Knowledge Ground*; for Monkey Baa: *The Peasant Prince*, *Possum Magic*; for Sydney Chamber Opera: *Breaking Glass*; and for Sydney Theatre Company: *The Effect*, *The Hanging*, *The Long Way Home*, *Muriel's Wedding the Musical*, *The Picture of Dorian Gray*. David was the Technical Director for *Griffin Lock-In* in 2020. David trained at NIDA and teaches for their graduate and postgraduate courses.

ISABELLA KERDIJK
STAGE MANAGER

Isabella graduated from the production course at the National Institute of Dramatic Art in 2008. She has worked as a stage manager and assistant stage manager on many shows, including: for Griffin: *And No More Shall We Part*, *Replay*, *The Smallest Hour*, *This Year's Ashes*, *Ugly Mugs*, *Wicked Sisters*; for Belvoir: *An Enemy of the People*, *The Dog/The Cat*, *The Drover's Wife*, *Every Brilliant Thing*, *Fangirls*, *Girl Asleep*, *The Glass Menagerie*, *HIR*, *Jasper Jones*, *Kill the Messenger*, *Mother*, *Mother Courage and Her Children*, *My Name is Jimi*, *Stories I Want to Tell You In Person* (National Tour), *The Sugar House*, *Thyestes* (European Tours), *Winyanboga Yurringa*; for Circus Oz: *Cranked Up*; for Darlinghurst Theatre Company: *Fourplay*, *Ride*, *Silent Night*; for Ensemble Theatre: *Rainman*, *The Ruby Sunrise*; for Legs on the Wall: *Bubble*; for LWAA: *The Mousetrap* (Australia/New Zealand Tours); for Spiegelworld: *Empire*. Isabella has worked as production coordinator on *Carmen* (Opera Australia on Sydney Harbour) and production manager/stage manager for *Puppetry of the Penis* (A-List Entertainment). She has also worked on various festivals, including The Garden of Unearthly Delights, Sydney Festival and the Woodford Folk Festival.

JOSEPH ALTHOUSE
EDDEN

Joseph 'Wunujaka' Althouse is a proud Tiwi/Arrernte man who lives and works on Gadigal Country. Joseph graduated from the National Institute of Dramatic Art with a BFA in 2018, where he was fortunate enough to be involved in productions including *The Changeling*, *Ex Machina*, *Salem* and *Stay Happy Keep Smiling*. Upon completing his studies, Joseph was privileged to play in Red Line Productions at the Old Fitz's production of *Angels in America*, where he won the Sydney Theatre Award for Best Male Actor in a Supporting Role in an independent production, for his portrayal of Belize. Joseph's other credits include: for Ensemble Theatre/Sydney Festival: *Black Cockatoo*; for Sydney Theatre Company: *Lord of the Flies*; and on screen: for the Australian Broadcasting Corporation: *Black Comedy*.
Joseph is delighted to make his Griffin debut in *Green Park*.

STEVE LE MARQUAND
WARREN

Steve's stage credits include: for Griffin: *Borderlines: The Return*, *Songket*, *Ugly Mugs*; for Belvoir: *An Enemy of the People*, *Buried Child*, *Death of a Salesman*, *Jasper Jones*, *Paul*, *The Spook*, *Summer of the Seventeenth Doll*, *Waiting for Godot*; for Darlinghurst Theatre Company: *Gaybies*; for Melbourne Theatre Company/Sydney Theatre Company: *Don's Party;* and for Sydney Theatre Company: *Holy Day*, *Gallipoli*, *The Serpent's Teeth*, *Tales From The Vienna Woods*, *The War of the Roses*. Steve also co-wrote, produced, directed and starred in the stage adaptation of *He Died With a Felafel in His Hand*. Steve's film credits include *A Few Best Men*, *Beneath Hill 60* (for which he earned a Film Critics Circle of Australia nomination for Best Supporting Actor), *Book Week*, *Broke*, *Escape and Evasion*, *June Again*, *Kill Me Three Times*, *Kokoda*, *Last Train to Freo* (for which he earned AFI and FCCA nominations for Best Lead Actor), *Locusts*, *Lost Things*, *Men's Group*, *Mullet*, *No Appointment Necessary*, *One Eyed Girl*, *Razzle Dazzle*, *Red Dog: True Blue*, *South Pacific*, *Terminus*, *Two Hands* and *Vertical Limit*. TV credits include: for the Australian Broadcasting Corporation: *G.P.*, *Janet King*, *Laid*, *Les Norton*, *Old School*, *Police Rescue*, *Rake*, *Riot*, *Wildside*; for Foxtel: *Wentworth*; for The Movie Network: *Small Time Gangster* (for which he earned an ASTRA nomination for Most Outstanding Actor); for Network 10: *Big Sky*; for Nine Network: *Farscape*, *Murder Call*, *Sea Patrol*, *Underbelly: Razor*, *Water Rats*, *Young Lions*; for Seven Network: *All Saints*, *Blue Heelers*, *Blue Murder: Killer Cop*, *Catching Milat*, *Home & Away*; and for Sky One: *Crash Palace*. He also won Best Actor at Tropfest in 1996 for his own short film *Cliché*.

ABOUT GRIFFIN

Griffin is the only theatre company in the country entirely devoted to new Australian plays. Located in the historic SBW Stables Theatre, nestled in the heart of bustling Kings Cross, Griffin has been a permanent home for the exploration of Australian stories since 1978.

Many of this country's most beloved and celebrated artists started out on our stage—Cate Blanchett, Michael Gow, Alma De Groen, David Wenham, to name a few—and iconic Australian plays like *The Boys*, *Holding the Man* and *City of Gold* had their world premieres at Griffin, before going out to capture the national imagination. We are a theatre of first chances.

We are passionate about nurturing emerging artists. We help ambitious, bold, risk-taking and urgent Australian plays get from a page onto a stage. We tell the stories that will help us know who we are as a nation, and who we want to become.

Stories about us. Written by us. For us.

Griffin Theatre Company and the SBW Stables Theatre operate and tell stories on the unceded lands of the Gadigal People of the Eora Nation. We acknowledge and honour Aboriginal and Torres Strait Islander people as the oldest continuous living culture on the planet, with more than 60,000 years of storytelling practice shaping and underpinning all aspects of Australian culture. It is a privilege that we do not take lightly: to work on this land, and to tell stories on its soil.

GRIFFIN THEATRE COMPANY
13 Craigend St
Kings Cross NSW 2011

02 9332 1052
info@griffintheatre.com.au
griffintheatre.com.au

SBW STABLES THEATRE
10 Nimrod St
Kings Cross NSW 2011

BOOKINGS
griffintheatre.com.au
02 9361 3817

GRIFFIN FAMILY

PATRON
Seaborn Broughton & Walford Foundation

Griffin acknowledges the generosity of the Seaborn, Broughton & Walford Foundation in allowing it the use of the SBW Stables Theatre rent free, less outgoings, since 1986.

BOARD
Bruce Meagher (Chair)
Simon Burke AO
Lyndell Droga
Tim Duggan
Declan Greene
Mario Philippou
Julia Pincus
Lenore Robertson
Simone Whetton
Meyne Wyatt

ARTISTIC
Artistic Director & CEO
Declan Greene

Associate Artistic Director
Tessa Leong

Associate Artist
Andrea James

Literary Associates
Julian Larnach
Poppy Tidswell

ADMINISTRATION
Interim Executive Director
Fiona Hulton

Associate Producer – Development
Frankie Greene

Associate Producer – Programming
Imogen Gardam

Associate Producer – Marketing
AJ Lamarque

Marketing Coordinator
Ang Collins

Marketing Assistant
Rebecca Abdel-Messih

Development Coordinator
Ell Katte

Program & Administration Coordinator
Whitney Richards

Strategic Insights Consultant
Peter O'Connell

PRODUCTION
Production Manager
Ryan Garreffa

Production Coordinator
Ally Moon

FINANCE
Finance Consultant
Tracey Whitby

Finance Manager
Kylie Richards

CUSTOMER RELATIONS
Box Office Manager
Dominic Scarf

Bar Manager
Grace Nye-Butler

Front of House
Ell Katte
Julian Larnach
Poppy Tidswell

Sustainability Coordinators
Ang Collins
Grace Nye-Butler

BRAND AND GRAPHIC DESIGN
Alphabet

COVER PHOTOGRAPHY
Brett Boardman

GRIFFIN DONORS

Income from Griffin activities covers less than 40% of our operating costs—leaving an ever-increasing gap for us to fill through government funding, sponsorship and the generosity of our individual supporters. Your support helps us bridge the gap and keep ticket prices affordable and our work at its best. To make a donation and a difference, contact Griffin on **9332 1052** or donate online at **griffintheatre.com.au**

COMPANY PATRONS
The Neilson Foundation
Merilyn Sleigh
& Raoul de Ferranti

PRODUCTION PATRON
The Girgensohn Foundation

PROGRAM PATRONS

Griffin Ambassadors
Robertson Foundation

Griffin Studio Ensemble
Mary Ann Rolfe

Griffin Studio
Gil Appleton
Darin Cooper Foundation
Kiong Lee & Richard Funston
Rosemary Hannah &
Lynette Preston
Ken & Lilian Horler
Pip Rath & Wayne Lonergan
Malcolm Robertson Foundation
Mary Ann Rolfe
Geoff & Wendy Simpson
Danielle Smith
Walking up the Hill Foundation

Griffin Women's Initiative
Griffin Women's Initiative is supported by Creative Partnerships Australia through Plus1

Katrina Barter
Wendy Blacklock
Christy Boyce & Madeleine Beaumont
Laura Crennan
Lyndell Droga
Melinda Graham
Sherry Gregory
Antonia Haralambis
Ann Johnson
Roanne Knox
Julia Pincus
Ruth Ritchie

Lenore Robertson
Sonia Simich
Margie Sullivan
Deanne Weir
Simone Whetton

SEASON PATRONS
As a new writing theatre, we program a wide range of stories that reflect our time, place and the unique voice of contemporary Australia. To ensure that these stories continue to be told, Griffin needs the help of private support to bring strength, insight, candour and new and powerful visions to the stage. Our Production Partner program is vital to our continued artistic success.

PRODUCTION PARTNERS 2020

Kindness by Matthew Whittet
Darin Cooper Foundation

SEASON DONORS

Front Row Donors +$10,000
Mary Ann Rolfe
Andrew Cameron AM & Cathy Cameron
Darin Cooper Foundation
Robert Dick & Erin Shiel
Gordon & Marie Esden
Stephen Fitzgerald
The Girgensohn Foundation
Rosemary Hannah & Lynette Preston
Belinda Hazelton & Vicki Archer
Ingrid Kaiser
Malcolm Robertson Foundation
Sophie McCarthy & Antony Green
Richard McHugh & Kate Morgan
Bruce Meagher & Greg Waters
Peter & Dianne O'Connell
Rebel Penfold-Russell OAM
Julia Pincus & Ian Learmonth

Pip Rath & Wayne Lonergan
Robertson Foundation
Mary Ann Rolfe
The Neilson Foundation
The Sky Foundation
Merilyn Sleigh & Raoul de Ferranti
The WeirAnderson Foundation
Kim Williams AM & Catherine Dovey

Main Stage Donor $5,000 - $9,999
Anonymous (1)
Antoniette Albert
Gil Appleton
Lisa Barker & Don Russell
Wendy Blacklock
Ellen Borda
Louise Christie
Bernard Coles
Lyndell & Daniel Droga
Danny Gilbert AM & Kathleen Gilbert
Ken & Lilian Horler
Kiong Lee & Richard Funston
Lee Lewis & Brett Boardman
David Marr & Sebastian Tesoriero
Catriona Morgan-Hunn
Don & Leslie Parsonage
Anthony Paull
Sue Procter
Geoff & Wendy Simpson
Danielle Smith & Sean Carmody
Walking Up the Hill Foundation

Final Draft $2,000-$4,999
Gae Anderson
Baly Douglass Foundation
Helen Bauer & Helen Lynch AM
Marilyn & David Boyer
Iolanda Capodanno
Alan Colletti
Bryony & Tim Cox
Lachlan Edwards
Elizabeth Fullerton

GRIFFIN DONORS

Kathy Glass
Jocelyn Goyen
GRANTPIRRIE/privare
James Hartwright &
Kerrin D'Arcy
Libby Higgin
Roanne & John Knox
Carina G. Martin
Janet Manuell
John McCallum & Jenny Nicholls
John Mitchell
David Nguyen
Chris Reed
Leslie Stern
Stuart Thomas
Tea Uglow
Richard Weinstein &
Richard Benedict

Workshop Donor $1,000-$1,999
Anonymous (4)
Michael Barnes
Katrina Barter
Cheery & Peter Best
Andrew Bell & Joanna Bird
Christy Boyce &
Madeleine Beaumont
Keith Bradley AM
Michael & Charmaine Bradley
Dr Bernadette Brennan
Jane Bridge
Corinne & Bryan
Stephen & Annabelle Burley
Susan Carleton
Adrian Christie
Sally Crawford
Laura Crennan
Nathan Croft & James White
Cris Croker & David West
Jane Curry
Timothy Davis
Carol Dettman
T Dolland & S McComb
Sue and Jim Dominguez
Christine Dunstan
Bob Ernst
Ros & Paul Espie
Brian Everingham
John & Libby Fairfax
Rowena Falzon
Robyn Fortescue &
Rosie Wagstaff
Jennifer Giles
Nicky Gluyas
Melinda Graham
Peter Gray & Helen Thwaites

Reg Graycar
Sherry Gregory
Antonia Haralambis
Judge Joe Harman
Kate Harrison
John Head
Danielle Hoareau
Mark Hopkinson &
Michelle Opie
Susan Hyde
Ann Johnson
Margaret Johnston
Deborah Jones
Jennifer Ledgar & Bob Lim
Richard & Elizabeth Longes
Chris Marrable &
Kate Richardson
Jane Munro
Elaine & Bill McLaughlin
Kent and Sandra McPhee
Joy Minter
Kate Mulvany
Tommy Murphy
John Nerthercoate
Ian Neuss & Penny Young
Patricia Novikoff
Ian Phipps
Martin Portus
Steve & Belinda Rankine
Judith & Frank Robertson
Sylvia Rosenblum
David & Dianne Russell
Sonia Simich
Jann Skinner
Geoffrey Starr
Robyn Stone
Adam Suckling & Pip McGuinness
Margie Sullivan
Peter Talbot
Mike Thompson
Sue Thomson
Daniel P. Tobin
Janet Wahlquist
Simone Whetton
Rosemary White
Paul & Jennifer Winch
Elizabeth Wing
Kathy Zeleny

Reading Donor $500-$999
Anonymous (3)
Brian Abel
Amity Alexander
Jes Andersen
Wendy Ashton
Robyn Ayres

Melissa Ball
Nikki Barrett
Penny Beran
Cherry & Peter Best
Phillip Black
Anne Britton
Annie Bourke
Larry Boyd & Barbara Caine AM
Simon Burke AO
Marianne Bush
Bill Calcraft
Gaby Carney
Jane Christensen
Amanda Clark
Eloise Curry
Melita Daru
David Davies
Michael Diamond
Max Dingle
Tim Duggan
David Earp
Wendy Elder
Leonie Flannery
Peter Graves
Erica Gray
Tonkin Zulaikha Greer
Edwina Guinness
Stephanie & Andrew Harrison
Mary Holt
David Hoskins & Paul McKnight
Sylvia Hrovatin
Marian & Nabeel Ibrahim
Mira Joksovic
David Jonas
Susan J Kath
Susan Kippax
David & Adrienne Kitching
Maruschka Loupis
Anne Loveridge
Ian & Elizabeth MacDonald
Robert Marks
Rebecca Massey
Christopher McCabe
Wendy McCarthy AO
Patrick McIntyre
Nicole McKenna
Paula McLean
Daniela McMurdo
Keith Miller
Stephen Mills
Neville Mitchell
Sarah Mort
William Peck
Carolyn Penfold
Judy Phillips

GRIFFIN DONORS

Malcolm Poole
Chris Puplick
Virginia Pursell
David Purves
Jennifer Rani
Alex-Oonagh Redmond
Annabel Ritchie
Jonquil Ritter
Roslyn Renwick
Colleen Roche
Karen Rodgers & Bill Harris
Gemma Rygate
Rob & Rae Spence
Mary Stollery & Eric Dole
Catherine Sullivan & Alexandra Bowen
Pearl Tan & Priya Roy
Ariadne Vromen
Jonathan Ware
John Waters
Rosemary White
William Zappa

First Draft Donor $200-$499
Anonymous (8)
Nicole Abadee & Rob Macfarlan
Priscilla Adey
Susan Ambler
Elizabeth Antonievich
Barbara Armitage
William Armitage
Chris Baker
Jan Barr
Edwina Birch
Rebecca Bourne Jones
Elizabeth Boyd
Shay Bristowe
Peter Brown
Dean Bryant & Mathew Frank
Wendy Buswell
Ruth Campbell
David Caulfield
Charlie Chan & Angela Catterns
Peter Chapman
Sue Clark
Amanda Connelly
Brendan Crotty & Darryl Toohey
Bryan Cutler
Owen Davies
Dora Den Hengst
Joanne & Sue Dalton
Susan Donnelly
Dr June Donsworth
Peter Duerden
Anna Duggan

Michele Dulcken
Kathy Esson
Elizabeth Evatt
Michael Eyers
Eamon Flack
Paul Fletcher
Helen Ford
Lee French
Matt Garrett
Sarah & Braith Gilchrist
Jock Given
Deane Golding
Thomas Gottlieb
Brenda Gottsche
Keith Gow
Hannah Grant
Virginia & Kieran Greene
Jo Grisard
Sue Hackett
Jennifer Hagan & Ron Blair
Glen Hamilton
Elizabeth Hanley
Carol Hargreaves
Raewyn Harlock
Grania Hickley
Stephanie Hui
Matthew Huxtable
C John Keightley
Maria Kelly
James Kelly & Beu Phuong
Catherine Kennedy
Penelope Latey
Peta Leemen
Karen Lee Smith
Antoinette Le Marchant
Caleb Lewis
Mark Lillis
Liz Locke
Norman Long
Dr Peter Louw
Carolyn Lowry
Anni Macdougall
Guillermo Martin
Katrina Matthews
Louise McDonald
Edward McGuiness
Duncan McKay
Ellen McLoughlin
Ian McMillan
Dr Steve McNamara
Sarah Miller
Bruce Milthorpe
Julia Mitchell
Catherine Moore
Pam Morris

Mullinars Casting Consultants
Dian Neligan
Carolyn Newman
Gennie Nevinson & Vivian Manwaring
Anthony Ong
Sally Patten
Susheela Peres Da Costa
Peter Pezzutti
Meredith Phelps
Belinda Piggott & David Ojerholm
Marion Potts
Christopher Powell
Janelle Prescott
Andrew Pringle
Steve Riethoff
Thelma Roach
In memory of Katherine Robertson
Ann Rocca
Catherine Rothery
Kevin and Shirley Ryan
Sharryn Ryan
Emily Scanlan
Julianne Schultz
Julia Selby
Diana Simmonds
Bridget Smith
Vanda & Martin Smith
Camilla Strang
The Steiner Family
Augusta Supple
Margot Tanjutco
Mark & Susan Tennant
Jane Theau
Elizabeth Thompson
Stephen Thompson
Susan Tiffin
Lawrence Vaux
Richard Vickery
Christophe Vivien
Belinda Wallington
Erik van Werven
Deanna Weir
Jennifer White
Ruth Wilson
Margaret Winn
Greg Wood
Eve Wynhausen
Robert Yuen
Aviva Ziegler

We would also like to thank Peter O'Connell for his expertise, guidance and time.

Current as of January 12 2021

SPONSORS

Government Supporters

Patron

Production Patron

GIRGENSOHN
FOUNDATION

Season Partner

Creative Partners

alphabet.

Company Sponsors

Griffin Theatre Company is assisted by the Australian Government through the Australia Council, its arts funding and advisory body; and the NSW Government through Create NSW.

www.ingramcontent.com/pod-product-compliance
Lightning Source LLC
Chambersburg PA
CBHW050026090426
42734CB00021B/3443